DISCOVER SERIES
GEMS

Gemas

Arete Ámbar Y Anillo

Amber Earring and Ring

Ágata Blanco y Negro

Black and White Agate

Ágate Azul

Blue Agate

Ágate Verde Azul

Blue Green Agate

Zafiro Azul

Blue Sapphire

Chacancanita

Chalcanthite

Citrina

Citrin

Cambio de Color Granate

Color-Change Garnet

Piedras Preciosas de Colores

Colorful Gemstones

Diamante

Diamond

Esmeralda

Emerald

Fluorita

Flourite

Collar de Cuentas Verdes

Green Beaded Necklace

Ónix

Onyx

Piedras Rosas y Azules

Pink and Blue Stones

Zafiro Rosa

Pink Sapphire

Piedras Preciosas

Precious Stones

Cuarzo Púrpura

Purple Quartz

Scapolite

Scapolite

Cuarzo Púrpura

Purple Quartz

Granate de Rodiolita

Rhodolite Garnet

Turmalina Rubellita

Rebellite Tourmaline

Rubí

Ruby

Aretes Serpentina

Serpentine Earrings

Obsidiana Copo de Nieve

Snowflake Obsidian

Make Sure to Check Out the Other Discover Series Books from Xist Publishing:

Published in the United States by Xist Publishing
www.xistpublishing.com
PO Box 61593 Irvine, CA 92602

© 2018 by Xist Publishing All rights reserved
Translated by Victor Santana
No portion of this book may be reproduced without express permission of the publisher
All images licensed from Fotolia
First Bilingual Edition

ISBN: 978-1-5324-0633-1   eISBN: 978-1-5324-0635-5

xist Publishing